THE TONY HART
ART FACTORY · 3

KAYE & WARD · LONDON

Introduction

There are projects in this book, the third in the series of four, that bring about designs, patterns and pictures that require no paper. For instance, a picture made entirely from little bits of scrap metal material. You'll have to make a collection of things like paper fasteners, paper clips, nails, screws, bits of oven foil – don't go out and buy them; find them. It's surprising how the shapes of these things will start giving you ideas as to how to use them. You'll see what I mean as you look through the book. Did you know that you can use wire to make a model, actually using it like modelling clay? There are many thicknesses of wire and each can have a different use in your picture making.

Light, in one form or another, is necessary in any picture. Sometimes we use dark and light paint on paper, simply to see which part is in shadow and which in the light. Some things, like polished wood, glass and brass pots are so shiny that they reflect light back to our eyes, like a mirror. You can make pictures like this too, using metallic paint, oven foil or silver paper.

Patterns are designs that repeat themselves here and there. Usually rather satisfying to do. Some people who say they are not artists often design excellent patterns. You'll find a lot of this sort of design in the book. To cut up an existing design to make yet another is fun and sometimes surprising. The world is full of patterns – keep your eyes open for them.

Metal, light
and patterns

METAL

The Owl Family – print from metal

It's worth collecting small metal objects from which to make prints. The varying shapes of washers, nuts, staples and nails lend themselves to imaginative prints. A piece of foam rubber, soaked in water-based printing ink, is ideal for inking up the metal.

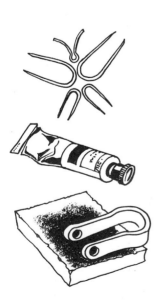

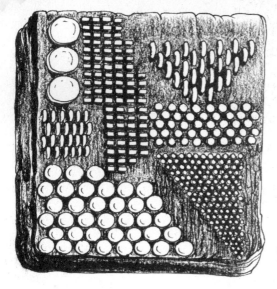

Nail collage

Some nails with interesting heads suitable for making a collage.

Choose a wood base that will not split when a great number of nails are hammered into it. You can drill suitable holes first, which will prevent splitting, or use cork. An old cork bathmat or several tablemats stuck together will do. Cork found on beaches is also good.

Metal foil, oven foil and silver paper are useful for making collages.

Moveable profile from coin and key chain

Metal assemblage

Viking ship from metal foil, nails, cup hooks and paper fasteners. The background is oven foil. Cut foil with old scissors. Foil can be scored to create lines and angles.

For heavier metal cutting use tin shears, wire cutters and a hacksaw. Ask an adult to help you with cutting and sawing, and beware! – when tin is cut it has *very* sharp edges. Wire profiles can be bent from coat-hangers and mounted on a wooden block.

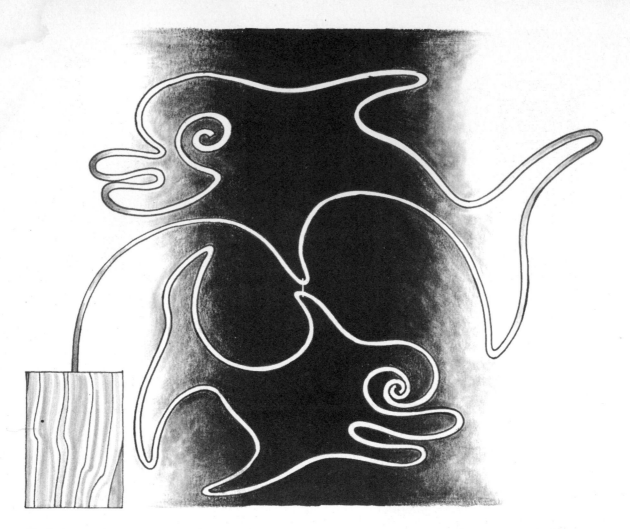

Dolphins shaped from coat-hanger wire.
Straighten the wire first and clean with a
household abrasive to make the metal shine.

Two lengths of galvanised wire bent in gentle
curves to form a sculpture. The four ends are
planted in four holes in a wood block. For a really
beautiful wire sculpture use 4 mm copper wire.
You buy it in rods approximately 2 metres long.

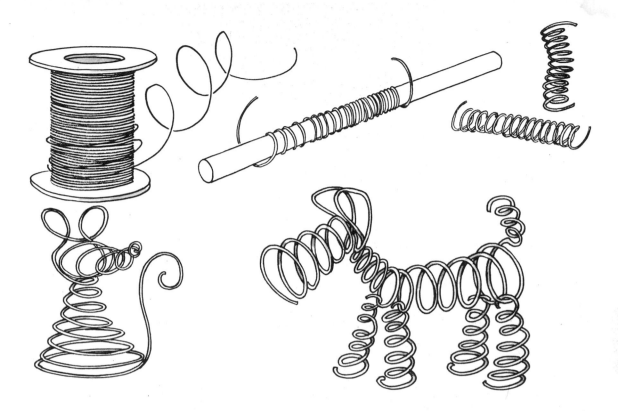

Wire sculpture

Plastic-coated wire and florists' wire can be used to shape free-standing figures. Fine wire can be crumpled and used like clay to shape forms.

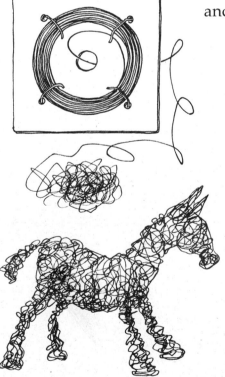

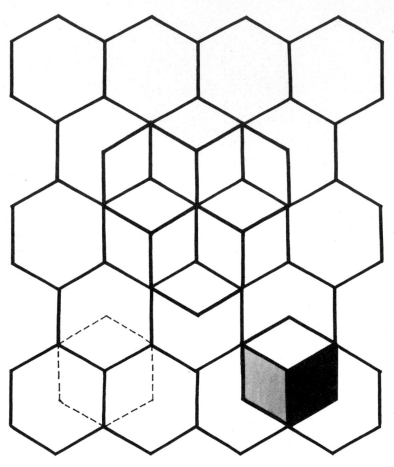

Chicken wire can be obtained with various sizes of mesh. It is generally galvanised and rust proof.

The hexagon is a six-sided shape. It provides an interesting pattern when interlocked and forms cubes when overlapped.

Crumpled and moulded by hand, chicken wire can be used to create three-dimensional forms.

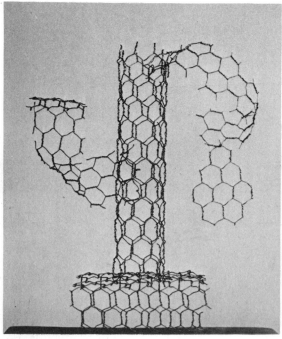

Transparent designs

Overlapping transparent material brings about new forms and new tones or colours. The three primary colours, red, yellow and blue, when overlapped show seven colours. See colour picture on page **3.16**.

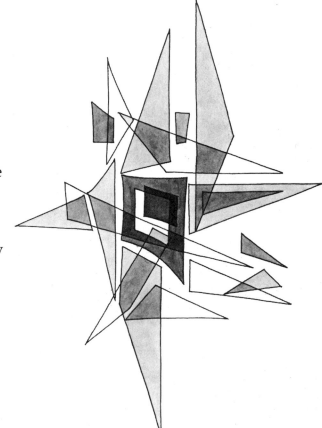

Coloured gels (acetate film or gelatine sheets) are used in theatre lighting. A collage made by overlapping scraps of these is effective if stuck on transparent material and placed in the window or with a light at the back. Stick with all-purpose clear adhesive.

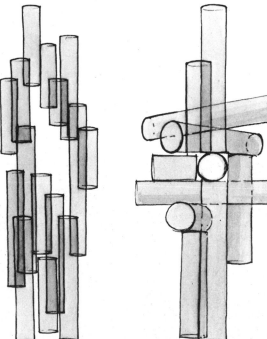

Gels rolled into tubes can be stuck with double-sided adhesive tape. Stuck to each other you can design a transparent tubular structure.

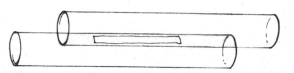

Cartoons and backgrounds

Acetate film is a clear, transparent material used by
cartoon film animators. Draw with indian ink on one
side. Turn over and colour with acrylic or poster paint.
This ensures that the black outline is sharp. The ink
drawing should be traced from your original pencil
drawing which can be quite rough.

Your painted drawing on film can now be placed over various backgrounds.
Here are two drawn textured backgrounds and a photograph.

Shiny relief pictures

Design a picture or pattern that can be cut out and stuck down on card so that all the bits are raised about 1 mm. You can add detail by scoring grooves into the card bits with a sharp piece of wood – not too sharp or it will tear the card.

Paint over the entire picture with matt black paint, poster colour or emulsion. When the paint is quite dry rub over with a soft cloth. Where you rub, the paint will shine. For a metallic shiny finish there is a metal paint in tubes that you can rub on, then polish.

Cover every bit with matt black paint.

Rub the metallic paint on with your finger.

Windows and light

Try exploding a simple shape like this. The design can be used as an unusual window. Coloured paper or 'gel' should be stuck on the back of these window designs. Painting the front of the window with a mixture of emulsion paint and sand gives it an appearance of stone. Do this before you stick the coloured material on the back.

Circular windows can be designed by folding and cutting paper first.

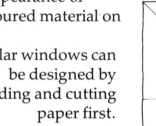

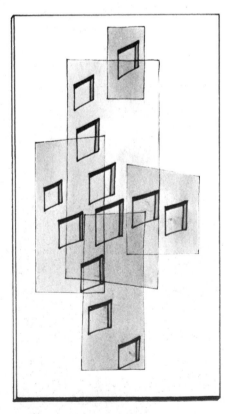

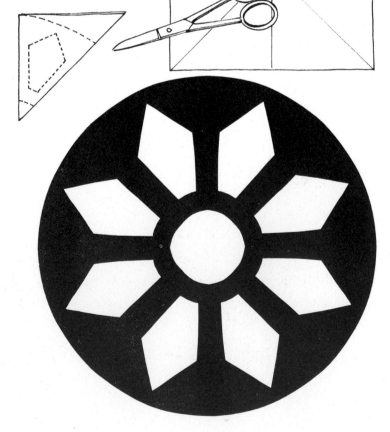

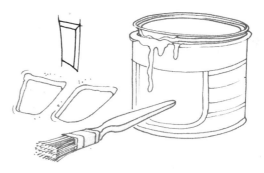

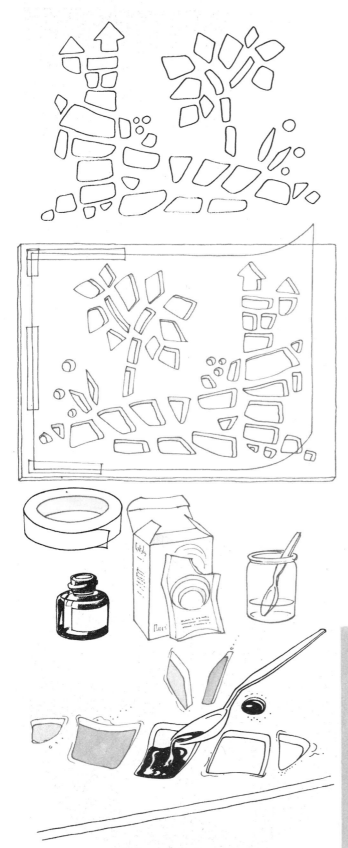

Simulated stained glass

Continuing the window theme, design a picture like a simple mosaic on thick card. Cut out all the shapes. Paint the card with sand-textured paint. When dry, reverse the card and stick clear acetate film to the back. This can be done with double-sided or ordinary clear adhesive tape.

Make up a very stiff gelatine mixture using household gelatine. About one teaspoon of gelatine to 2 teaspoons of hot water. When the gelatine has dissolved, mix in a few drops of coloured ink – ink, not paint. When it cools and starts to set, pour it into the window depressions. Use as many colours as you wish. The result looks like very thick coloured glass.

Decorated foil

Metal foil can be engraved by drawing into the surface with a wooden stylus. Put a few newspapers under the metal foil to protect the table and to obtain a deeper groove. Left this way the design will be sunken. Turn the foil over and the design will be raised.

You can paint the foil with black poster paint and, when dry, rub it with fine sandpaper. It gives the whole thing an antique look!

Try taking a wax crayon rubbing from the design.

Foil figures

Foil of this sort can be cut from the containers used in Chinese and Indian "take away" meals. A collage using cut and scored foil is shown against a background of rough hessian and corrugated card. The contrast between rough and smooth is always effective.

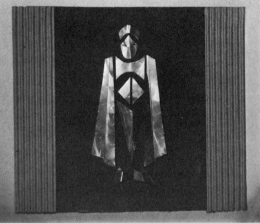

The chessman figure and bull are made by folding and rolling the flat sheet of foil after cutting it. When curving foil, do it by rolling it against something round otherwise you will get a series of crinkles.

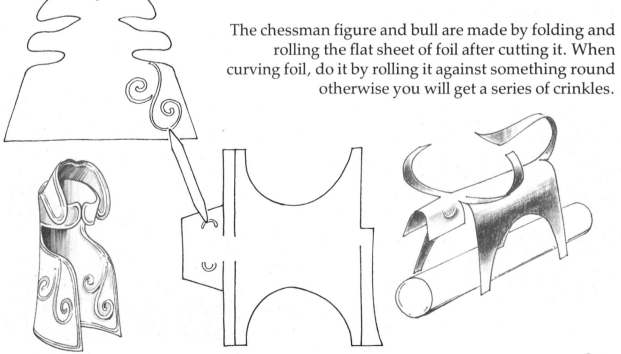

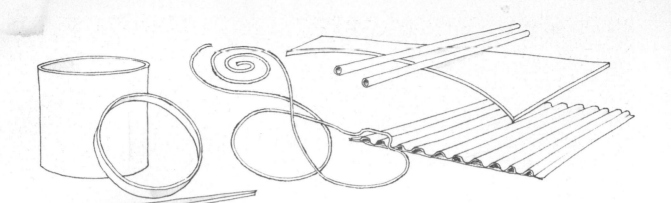

Simulated metal relief

You can make anything look like metal by covering it with metal paint. Even bits of rubbish can be transformed by doing this. The card background is covered with shapes cut from plastic netting, corrugated cardboard, drinking straws, a section of cardboard tube and bits of string. When a design emerges the bits are stuck down. Spilt glue makes its own pattern if you drag cardboard through it! Now paint it with metallic paint. This you can do with a brush and gold leaf paint or spray it with a metallic aerosol spray.

Metallic bits and pieces make light
reflective collages and assemblages.

Dolphins from two wire coat
hangers.

Drawing on transparent film can be positioned and repositioned over any sort of background.

Three primary colours overlap to make seven in all.

Coloured acetate film cut and overlapped to form a transparent collage.

Metallic paint on piped tube adhesive.

Burnished
metallic
paint
on card
relief
design.

(*above*) Cut paper mosaic. Light card and water colour.

(*above right*) Folded and cut black paper over ink splashed white card.

Beans and seeds stuck to thick cardboard.

Material collage. All pieces can be repositioned to alter design.

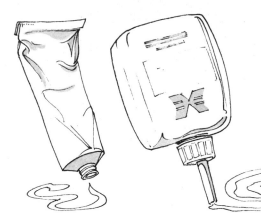

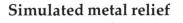

Simulated metal relief

Squeeze glue shapes onto card. Use Universal or contact adhesive. When dry, spray with black paint from one direction. Then spray with metallic paint from the other direction. Or simply paint with gold leaf paint. Cut shapes out and rearrange on a dark or bright coloured background. Metallic gold shapes look good against red card.

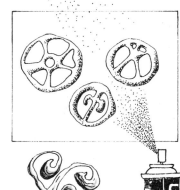

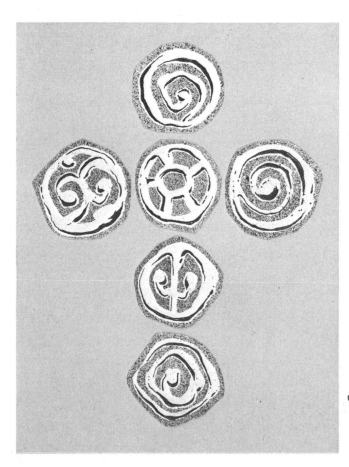

String

String patterns

A universal adhesive spread thickly on a card base will remain tacky long enough for a string pattern to be stuck down. It can also be used as a block from which to make a print.

With a complicated string pattern, use the adhesive in small areas and put the string down a little at a time.

The background can be painted card or hessian stuck on card.

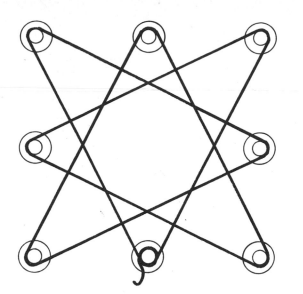

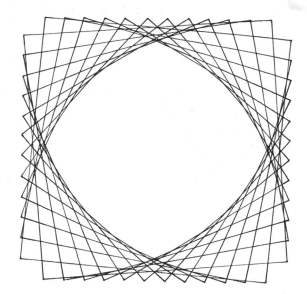

Geometric patterns can be made by wrapping string round a series of drawing pins or nails. The effect of curves can be made but only straight lines are used.

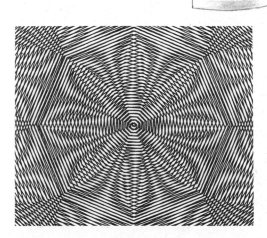

Pin a cardboard cut-out to a piece of card and trace the shape with a pen. Move the shape on and trace again. Repeat until a satisfying pattern is produced.

This pattern could be made by hand, given time. In this case a computer did the job in a fraction of the time.

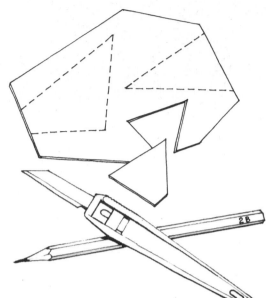

Reflected patterns

A shape cut from another shape and turned over brings about a reflecting pattern, the spaces being part of the pattern.

Cutting a shape into bits and moving the bits will bring about a design. This process is called 'exploding' because the pieces are moved outwards from the middle.

Drip stencils

Make a simple design by dripping washing-up liquid onto white card or paper. Spray paint over the design, or use a toothbrush and nail to stipple. The paint or ink must be permanent.

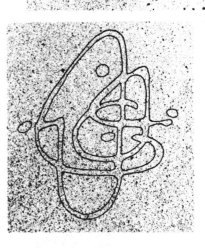

Drip more washing-up liquid to continue the design. Spray over again. Wash under tap and leave to dry.

Mobiles

The only difficulty about making a mobile is to make it balance. The suspended objects are best made from materials that can be added to or from which bits can be removed. Cardboard, art straws, tin foil do well. Plasticine is good but heavier.

Balance is achieved by moving the threads from which the mobile objects are suspended.

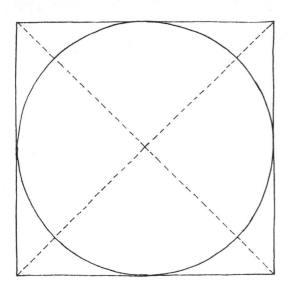

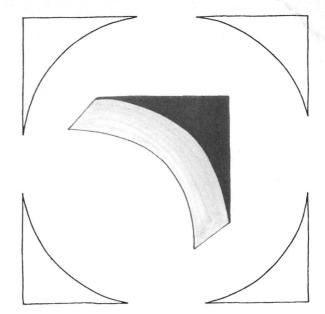

Repeat patterns

The simplest and most effective pattern is made from a circle and a square. Just one corner is used to make hundreds of patterns. Make a little block from polystyrene, wood, rubber or cardboard. Ink up from an ink pad and start printing. The examples have been used for floor tiles. See how many more you can make.

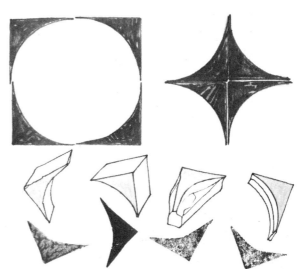

Relief panel

This relief panel is made by cutting two thicknesses of cardboard into small shapes and sticking them to a card background. The thickness of the pieces causes deep shadows and it's interesting to hold the finished work at different angles to the light to see the different effects. Paint it an overall matt white or light colour as this will give the most satisfying lighting effect.

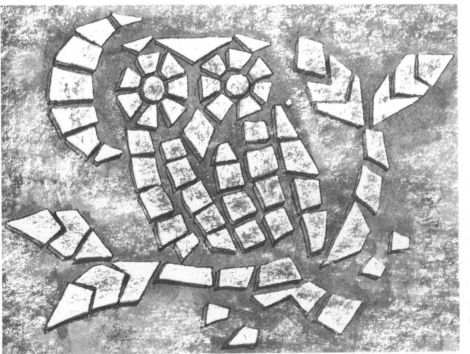

Also suitable for metallic paint.

For use as a printing block.

From which to make a rubbing.

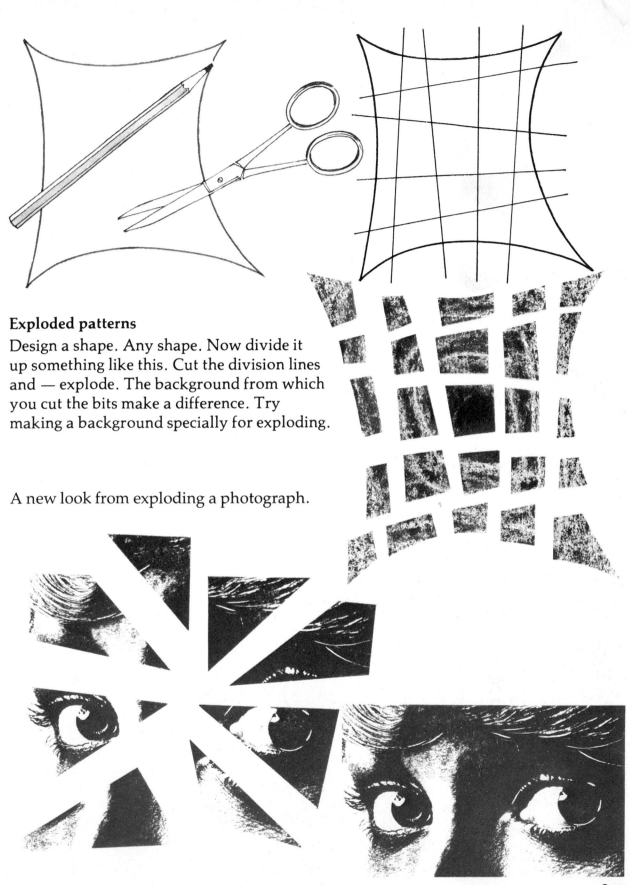

Exploded patterns

Design a shape. Any shape. Now divide it
up something like this. Cut the division lines
and — explode. The background from which
you cut the bits make a difference. Try
making a background specially for exploding.

A new look from exploding a photograph.

Paper mosaic

Colour cartridge paper with paint or ink. Use a coarse brush and allow the paint to streak a bit, let one colour run into another.

When dry, cut the paper into strips, and the strips into small squares. Don't make perfect squares! It's *not* being perfect squares that gives character to this sort of mosaic.

You can create a picture that is entirely covered with little squares (colour picture on page **3**.18) or do something like this.

Seeds and beans

Here seeds are used as units for a highly textured mosaic. This kind of work is most satisfying, though time consuming.

Choose about half a dozen different sizes, shapes and colours of seeds and beans. Stick them down onto a really thick piece of cardboard or hardboard. Use clear adhesive or multi-purpose glue. When sticking down large areas of small seeds, glue the whole area and try to get all the seeds down before it dries! The seeds that I find most useful are: black and white peppercorns, white haricot beans, lentils, split peas and sunflower seeds.

Pebbles and stone

Pebbles, worn smooth by the sea, are used to make paths. By using black and white pebbles, patterns are made. You could do the same thing with white beans. Paint beans black by putting paint and beans in a plastic bag and shaking them up. Plant the beans in modelling clay.

A Romano-British mosaic.
About 9,500 pieces of stone are shown here.

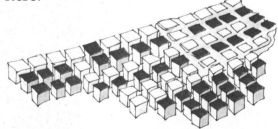

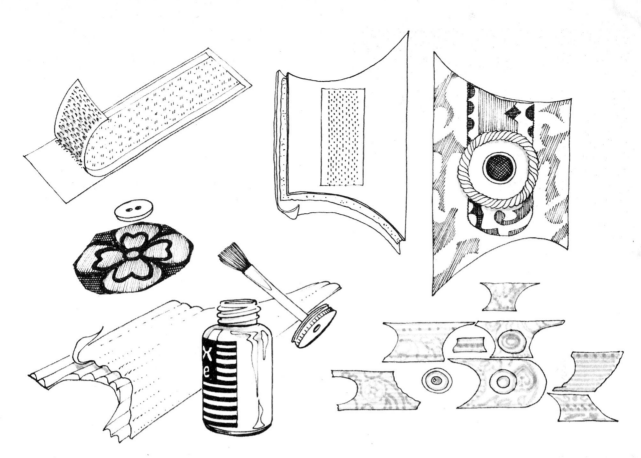

Material collage

When cloth and other fabrics are used in a collage it is useful to be able to reposition the pieces. Drapers' shops stock a tape that will attach itself to woolly materials but can be detached. Here I have used bits from the rag bag, stuck with latex adhesive to card, foam rubber and corrugated card bases. As a wall hanging you can alter the design whenever you like.

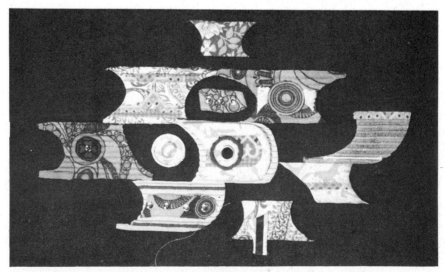

Patterns from bricks

Some complicated patterns emerge from both the two shapes and two colours. Most patterns are made from just the two shapes. The long shape – the stretcher, and the short shape – the header. You can design brick patterns by printing the individual brick shapes from a home-made block. Another method is to cut paper bricks and 'lay' them. Complicated patterns are best drawn in pencil first on a grid.

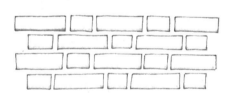

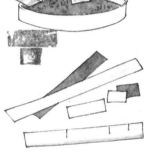

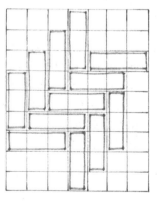

Rusty metal sculpture

This should only be undertaken with great care as cuts or scratches from rusty metal can be dangerous. If you want to try this it is a good idea to wear gloves. There is a lot of this scrap about. The texture and colour is often most satisfying. It can be cut easily with tin shears and stuck with epoxy resin adhesive. Brush away surplus rust particles with a wire brush. Varnish if you want it to shine.

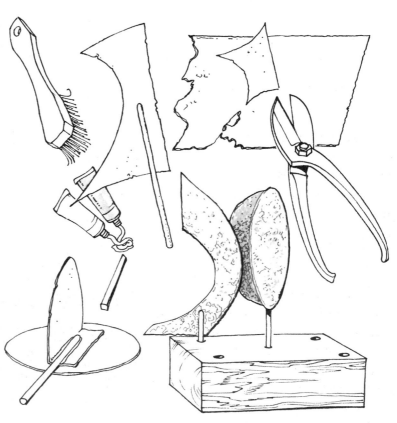

Real texture

Make up some wallpaper paste. On a suitable surface – a laminated plastic top – lay a sheet of newspaper. Brush paste all over it and put down a second sheet of newspaper. Repeat this until you have a pile of six sheets of newspaper, the top one pasted too. With your fingers, push, prod and pull the newspaper until you have produced a series of whorls and ridges. Leave to dry. It takes some time with thick papier-mâché.

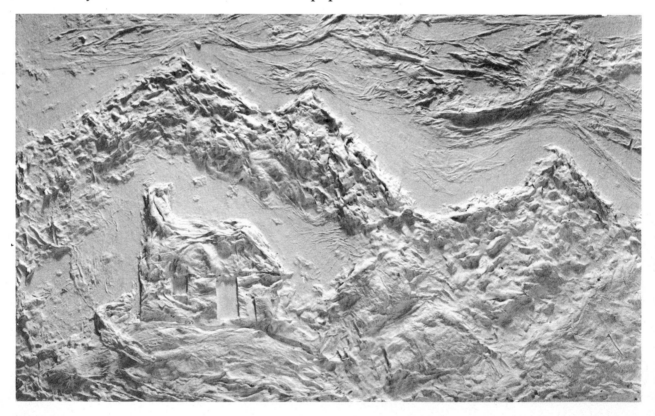

First published by Kaye & Ward Ltd
Century House, 82/84 Tanner Street, London SE1 3PP
1980

ISBN 0 7182 1265 7

Typeset by John Smith, London
Printed in Great Britain by
The Fakenham Press Ltd, Fakenham, Norfolk